J   4630266B
796.357   Jensen, Julie, 1957-
JEN   Beginning softball

D1405068

BALL GROUND PUBLIC LIBRARY
435 OLD CANTON ROAD
BALL GROUND, GA 30107

SEQUOYAH REGIONAL LIBRARY

3 8749 0046 3026 6

Beginning
SOFTBALL

Coach Fred Wroge and the
following athletes were
photographed for this book:
    Tamara Anderson,
    Molly Chirico,
    Rachael Ekholm,
    Kathryn Hafertepe,
    Colleen Hinz,
    Dupe Omoyayi,
    Tripper Teslow,
    Katie Wells,
    Katie White,
    Leah Zarn.

Beginning
SOFTBALL

Julie Jensen

Adapted from Kristin Wolden Nitz's
Fundamental Softball

Photographs by Andy King

THIS BOOK IS THE PROPERTY OF
SEQUOYAH REGIONAL LIBRARY
CANTON, GEORGIA

Lerner Publications Company
Minneapolis

To the 1996 Lady Hawks

Copyright © 1997 by Lerner Publications Company

All rights reserved. International copyright secured. No part of this book may be reproduced or transmitted in any form or by any means, electronic or mechanical, including photocopying and recording, or by any information storage or retrieval system, without permission in writing from Lerner Publications Company, except for the inclusion of brief quotations in an acknowledged review.

Library of Congress Cataloging-in-Publication Data

Jensen, Julie, 1957–
  Beginning softball / Julie Jensen ; adapted from Kristin Wolden
Nitz's fundamental softball ; photographs by Andy King.
    p. cm.— (Beginning sports)
  Includes bibliographical references and index.
  Summary: Provides an introduction to both slow- and fast-pitch
softball, covering the history, basic skills, rules, equipment, and
terminology of the sport.
  ISBN 0-8225-3510-6 (alk. paper)
  1. Softball—Juvenile literature. [1. Softball.] I. King,
Andy, ill. II. Nitz, Kristen Wolden. Fundamental softball.
III. Title. IV. Series.
GV881.25.J45 1997
796.357'8—dc21   96-45201

Manufactured in the United States of America
1 2 3 4 5 6 – JR – 02 01 00 99 98 97

The Beginning Sports series was designed in conjunction with the Fundamental Sports series to offer young athletes a basic understanding of various sports at two reading levels.

Photo Acknowledgments
Photographs are reproduced with the permission of: p. 8, The Hennepin County Historical Society; pp. 9, 51, ALLSPORT/Jamie Squire; pp. 10, 16 (both) © Peter Ford; p. 11, Photo courtesy of Sports Vision 20/20.

Diagrams and artwork by Laura Westlund.

Contents

Chapter 1 . . . . . How This Game Got Started 7
Chapter 2 . . . . . The Basics 13
Chapter 3 . . . . . Fielding and Throwing 23
Chapter 4 . . . . . Pitching 39
Chapter 5 . . . . . Hitting and Running 53
Chapter 6 . . . . . Taking the Field 65
Softball Talk 77
Further Reading 78
Index 79

How This Game Got Started

In summer, many people head for the softball field. They gather their friends and split into teams. Some players play in backyards. Others use fields at city parks. Sometimes, high school and college teams play in stadiums. Cheering fans watch the top-level games.

Softball began in 1887 on Thanksgiving Day. A group of young men was gathered at Chicago's Farragut Boat Club for the holiday. Miles away, the college football teams of Harvard and Yale universities were playing a game. Some of the young men in Chicago were cheering for Harvard. Others were rooting for Yale. The men followed the game by reading telegrams. When the last telegram came in, the group learned that Yale had won. A happy Yale fan playfully threw a boxing glove at the Harvard group. A Harvard fan swung at the glove with a stick. He hit the glove back over the Yale fan's head. That gave one of the men, George Hancock, an idea. He suggested that they play ball. He tied the glove into a lumpy ball by using the laces. He used chalk to draw bases on the gym floor.

For the next hour, the teams played this new kind of baseball. They scored 80 runs! Hancock and his friends had fun that afternoon. Hancock had so much fun that he offered to write down rules. Each Saturday night, Hancock and his friends played their new

Lewis Rober, a firefighter in Minnesota, refined the game of softball and took it outdoors.

game. They called it *Indoor Base Ball* and they told other people about it too. By the end of that winter, people all over Chicago were playing.

People in other parts of the country learned about the new game. One of those people, a Minnesota fireman named Lewis Rober, moved the game outdoors. He wanted his firefighters to get some exercise while they weren't fighting fires. In 1895, Rober set up a field in a vacant lot outside his firehouse. Rober's game was a lot like indoor baseball. It could be played on a small field since the ball didn't travel far. A full game could be played in an hour. That hour was full of fun!

People across the country played this new kind of baseball in different ways. Each region made up its own rules. Even the equipment was different. The ball could be anything from 10 to 20 inches around. The names were different too. Some people called their game *mush ball*. Others played *pumpkin ball*. By the 1920s, most people were using the name *softball.*

Dot Richardson played shortstop for the 1996 U.S. gold-medal softball team.

Doctor Dot

Sometimes athletes have to have surgery. One famous athlete knows how to perform surgery. Most medical students go straight to bed after a long shift. Instead, Dot Richardson works out. It's not easy being a shortstop and a surgeon.

Dot took a year off medical school to play in the 1996 Olympic Games. She was a shortstop on the U.S. team. Dot's team won the gold medal.

Dot first started playing baseball. She switched to softball when she was 10. She played in a women's league. Three years later, she joined the national Women's Major Fast Pitch League. She was the youngest player in the league. Since then, Dot has won seven Golden Glove awards.

People of all ages all over the world play softball for fun and exercise.

Once, the only games girls were allowed to play were non-contact sports like croquet, tennis, and badminton. But girls and women wanted to play this new game too. By 1926, women were playing the fast-paced game that modern college athletes do.

The first national softball tournament was held at the 1933 Chicago World's Fair. More than 350,000 people watched teams of men and women in the three-day tournament. The fans then took softball back home with them.

The game spread across the nation.

Leo Fischer was a reporter who wrote about the world's fair tournament. After the fair, he helped to start the Amateur Softball Association (ASA). The ASA set standards for rules and equipment so that people from different parts of the country could play against each other.

There are still different kinds of softball games. In Chicago, players use a 16-inch ball, but they don't use gloves. In Maine and Alaska, people play in the snow. In Washington and Idaho, some players play while wearing snowshoes. Players play in the sand in California. They don't use gloves and they don't run the bases.

The most popular forms of softball are fast-pitch and slow-pitch. These games are played all across the country. The best fast-pitch players can throw the ball as fast as a Major League Baseball pitcher. Fast-pitch pitchers put **stuff** on the ball to make it rise, drop, or curve as it gets to the plate. Fast-pitch softball is often a low-scoring game. Good fast-pitch pitchers can keep all but the best batters from getting a hit.

The pitcher's job in slow-pitch softball is to lob the ball across the plate with a high **arc.** Hitting a pitch like that can be difficult. Still, there is much more hitting and fielding in slow-pitch softball.

The ASA puts on national tournaments for both fast-pitch and slow-pitch players. Fast-pitch softball is what high school and college athletes play on school teams. Fast-pitch softball is also popular at the international level.

Special Rules for Special Players

In beep baseball, players who can't see are teamed with players who can. The sighted players pitch and catch for their teammates.

The pitcher shouts "Ready" when the ball leaves his or her fingers. The pitcher then yells "Ball" just when the batter should swing. A beeper in the ball also helps the batter.

Once a batter hits the ball, a scorekeeper punches a button. That starts one of two 4-foot pylons buzzing. These are the bases. They are located along the first and third base lines. The batter listens to whichever pylon is buzzing. Then he or she runs toward the sound. Six fielders are listening closely too. They must field the beeping ball. If the batter makes it to the base before a fielder gets the ball, the batter scores a run. If a fielder gets the ball first, the batter is out.

Chapter 2

THE BASICS

As the Amateur Softball Association says, softball is a sport for everyone. Players begin by hitting balls off a tee. Then, a coach pitches to the batters. Soon, the players are pitching to each other.

Some players keep playing as they grow older. Some play fast-pitch softball for school teams. They play in high school and college games. Other players play slow-pitch in recreational leagues. Players at all levels try hard to do their best—and to have a good time!

Each league and every level has special rules. Despite these small differences in equipment and field size, the game is still softball.

The pitcher's rubber

The batter's boxes on either side of home plate

The Field of Play

The field is in the shape of a square. One of the points of the square is home plate. Because most of the fans look at the field from behind home plate, the square looks like a diamond. That's why a ball field is often called a *diamond*. Home plate, where the batter stands, is the base of the diamond. The raked dirt around the bases is called the **infield**. The grassy region beyond is the **outfield**.

The **pitcher's rubber** is between home plate and second base. The distance between the pitcher's rubber and home plate depends on the league. Foul lines start at the pointed back of home plate. The lines run along the outer edges of first and third base and go out to the fence. A batted ball that lands between those two lines is a fair ball. A batted ball that first hits the ground outside those lines is a **foul ball**. On some fields, the lines are marked in chalk. On others, the umpires have to use their judgment to decide whether a hit is fair or foul.

Distances Table

Fast-pitch

Division	Distance between bases	Distance from pitcher's rubber to home plate
ages 10 and under	55'	35'
girls 12 and under	60'	35'
boys 12 and under	60'	40'
girls 18 and under	60'	40'
boys 18 and under	60'	46'
Adult women	60'	40'
Adult men	60'	46'

Slow-pitch

Division	Distance between bases	Distance from pitcher's rubber to home plate
ages 10 and under	55'	35'
girls 12 and under	60'	40'
girls 14 and under	65'	46'
girls 18 and under	65'	50'
boys 12 and under	60'	40'
boys 14 and under	65'	46'
boys 18 and under	65'	50'
Adult	65'	50'

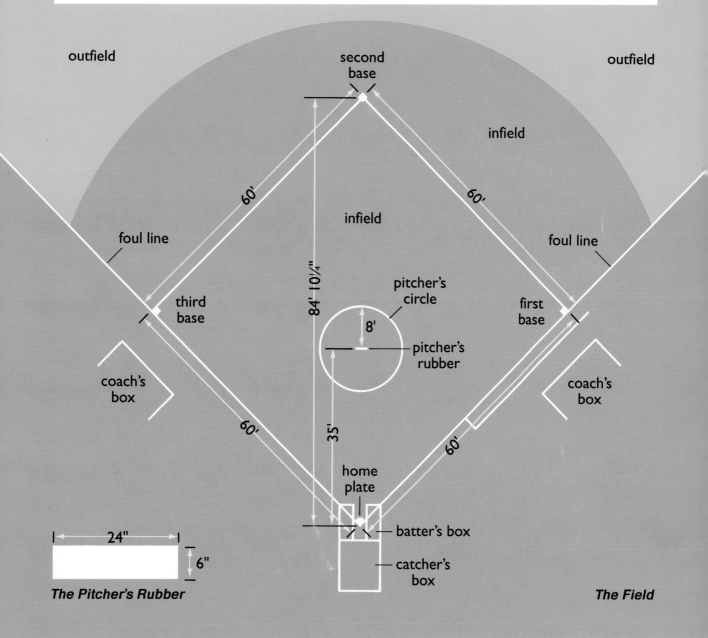

The Pitcher's Rubber

The Field

Equipment

● *The Ball*

A softball isn't really soft. In the middle of the ball, there is a center core made of cork, rubber, or fibers. Yarn is wound around this core. Then, a cowhide or synthetic cover is sewn around the ball.

Most softballs are 12 inches around. That's double the size of a baseball. Since a softball

weighs about 7 ounces, it weighs a little more than a baseball too. That's why a softball doesn't fly as far as a baseball does.

The 12-inch softball is the standard. Softballs come in many different sizes and colors, however. Different types of leagues use different types of balls. There are 11-inch balls for youth leagues.

● The Glove

The most important part of the glove is the **pocket.** The pocket is the part of the glove between the thumb and forefinger. The pocket needs to be large enough to catch a softball. Some baseball gloves have pockets that are too small for softball players.

Gloves get better as they get older because they get "broken in." This means the leather becomes more flexible. A glove can be broken in faster by rub-

bing it with a conditioner. To break in a new glove, a player might put a ball in the pocket after practice. Then, the player can use string or a rubber band to hold the ball in the pocket until the next practice.

A catcher's mitt, above, is bigger and doesn't have the individual finger spaces that a fielder's glove, below, does.

Batting helmets, at left, are hard plastic foam-lined hats that protect players while they're batting and running. Bats, at right, come in many sizes and colors.

● *The Bat*

Each bat has a handle, a barrel, and a knob. A batter grips the bat on the taped handle. The ball is hit with the barrel. The knob keeps the bat from slipping out of the batter's hands.

Bats can be made of wood or aluminum. An aluminum bat is lighter and lasts longer than a wooden one. Also, an aluminum bat won't break.

Some big bats have fancy names like "Bleacher-Reacher." The size of the bat isn't really that important. It is important to be able to swing the bat quickly. The faster you swing, the harder you hit the ball.

Try this to choose a bat. Pick up the bat by the knob with your weaker arm. Hold the bat straight out in front of you. If the bat sags down, use a lighter bat.

● *Other Equipment*

Many softball players wear running shoes or court shoes when playing. Some players wear special softball shoes. These shoes have rubber cleats to grip the ground.

Softball players often wear loose, comfortable clothes to practice. For games, players wear uniforms. The uniforms can be a T-shirt and shorts, or a jersey and short pants.

All batters and runners wear batting helmets. These hard plastic helmets prevent head injuries. A catcher must have a face mask, helmet, chest protector, and shin guards.

A catcher must wear protective gear in case he or she is hit by a ball or an incoming runner.

Shoes with cleats help players keep their footing on slippery outfield grass.

The Rules

During a game, the batter stands in a batter's box. The pitcher tries to throw the ball underhand through the batter's **strike zone.** The umpire decides if a pitch went through the strike zone.

The batter doesn't have to swing at the pitch. If the batter doesn't swing and the pitch doesn't go through the strike zone, the umpire will call the pitch a **ball.** If the batter doesn't swing and the pitch does go through the strike zone, the umpire will call the pitch a **strike.** If the batter swings at the pitch and misses, it's a strike. A batter can also get a strike by hitting the ball into foul territory.

If a pitcher throws four balls to a batter, the batter gets a **walk** to first base. If a pitcher throws three strikes to a batter, the batter makes an **out.** The number of balls and strikes a batter has is called the **count.**

Once the batter hits the ball into fair territory, the action starts. The batter becomes a runner and races to first base.

shoulders

armpits

slow-pitch strike zone

fast-pitch strike zone

knees

home plate

Strike Zones

The fielders can make a **force-out** by throwing the ball to first base before the runner can get there. The runner is out if the defensive player has the ball and is touching the base.

If there is another runner already on first base, the fielders might try to put out that runner instead. To do that, the fielders must get the ball to second base before the runner.

But a runner on second base doesn't have to run when the ball is hit if there's not a runner on first. In that case, the fielder must **tag** the runner to get the out. If the runner heads to third, the fielder at third base has to touch the runner with the ball. The fielders can also tag a runner if he or she isn't on a base.

A fielder can also put out the batter by catching a **fly ball** before it hits the ground.

When a player makes it all the way around the bases without being tagged or forced out, that player scores a run. Each team bats until it makes three outs. An inning is completed when both teams have batted.

FIELDING AND THROWING

Like most games, softball has many rules. There are also special skills and moves to learn if you want to play the game well. But learning to be a fielder isn't complicated. The basic moves really come down to two things: stopping the ball and getting it to the right place.

Fielding

● Fly Balls

There's a secret to catching a fly ball. The secret is: you have to watch the ball from the instant it leaves the bat until it smacks into your glove.

Molly is catching a fly ball in the photo on the next page. When the ball is hit, Molly runs to where she thinks the ball will come down. As she runs, she calls out "I've got it!"

Catching a tennis ball with your bare hands is a good way to practice.

Catching the Ball

You have to catch the ball before you can make the play. Sounds pretty basic, right? It is, but even very good players make this mistake. Many players have dropped the ball because they were thinking about making the tag. Remember, catch the ball first. Here's another basic rule to remember: Use both hands when catching the ball. That may sound like a rule just for beginners, but it's not. Trapping the ball in your glove with your bare hand will keep it from falling out.

23

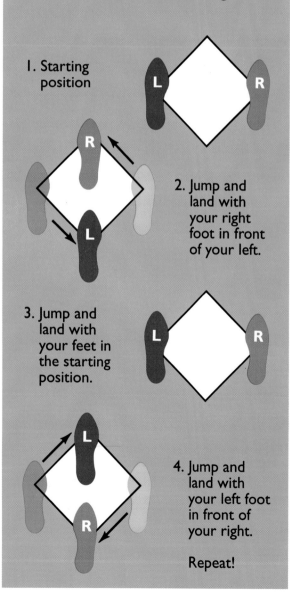

Diamond Drill

Doing the diamond drill can improve your speed, agility, and conditioning. To do the drill, start with your feet about shoulder width apart. Follow the steps below. Start by doing the drill slowly. Then speed up until you're going at full speed. Rest for a few seconds and then do the diamond drill again.

1. Starting position

2. Jump and land with your right foot in front of your left.

3. Jump and land with your feet in the starting position.

4. Jump and land with your left foot in front of your right.

Repeat!

Once Molly gets underneath the ball, she lifts her glove above her eyes. She holds the glove with its fingers pointing up. As the ball thuds into the pocket, Molly covers the ball with her other hand.

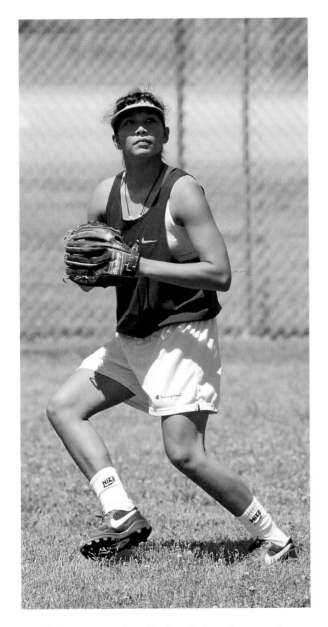

When a ball is hit deep into the outfield, Rachael turns and runs while watching the ball over her shoulder. She catches the ball over her shoulder.

Softball players try to get under a fly ball and get in front of a **ground ball**.

● Ground Balls

A ball bouncing on the ground can move in strange ways. The fielder wants to stop the ball with the glove. But if the ball hops over the glove, the fielder has to block the ball with his or her body. If the ball is in front of the fielder's body, the player can pick it up and throw it quickly. If the ball gets behind the fielder, the player has to turn around and chase the ball. That takes up time.

In the photos on this page, Tripper shows how to field the ball. His feet are wide apart and his knees are bent. His glove is open and touching the dirt. Tripper moves in front of the ball. He puts the tip of his glove to the ground so the ball won't roll under it. Tripper watches the ball until it is in his glove. Then he covers the ball with his bare hand to keep it from bouncing out.

If the ball is rolling slowly on the dirt, an infielder can run toward it. Kathy is running to meet the ball in the photos on the next page. By running to the ball, she will reach it faster and her throw will be shorter.

Off the Wall

Throw a tennis ball against a wall. Throw it at different angles, heights, and speeds. Practice stopping different kinds of grounders.

● *Line Drives*

A **line drive** is a fast, hard-hit ball. It doesn't leave a fielder much time to react. Kathy knows that when a line drive is above her waistline, she should catch the ball with her glove pointing up. That's what she did in the photo at left.

When the line drive is below her belt, she catches it with her fingers pointing down, as in the photo below.

Warmups

Smart players warm up first. Many teams begin practice by jogging around the outside of the softball field. This helps the players loosen up their muscles. Then, they stretch their muscles. When you stretch, remember:

1. Don't stretch so hard it hurts.

2. Don't hold your breath. Breathe normally.

3. Stretch both sides of your body.

Be sure to warm up your throwing arm. One good way to warm up your arm is to play catch on your knees.

Throwing

There are different ways to throw a ball. Each way is used for a certain situation. Each one begins with a good grip.

Hold the ball with your fingertips, not in your palm. Place your middle finger and forefinger where the seams come together. Put your thumb underneath the ball.

Fielders use the overhand throw to make a long throw.

● *Overhand*

Colleen shows how to throw overhand in the photos on this page and the next three pages. After Colleen catches the ball, she faces her target. Then she brings the ball down and behind her head.

She steps forward with her glove-hand leg. Her glove shoulder and hip point to her target. Her throwing arm is back and her wrist is cocked.

As her throwing arm comes forward, her elbow passes her ear. She shifts her weight forward as she lets go of the ball. Her hand follows the ball.

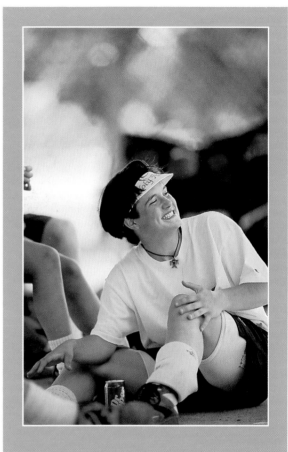

Wanted: Team Players

Have you ever heard someone say, "What a team player!" That's a great compliment for a softball player or any athlete. That means that player cares more about the team than his or her personal desires.

Being a team player means being ready to play. By eating right, getting enough rest, and stretching before you practice, you can stay ready to go.

Being a team player also means listening to the coach. Each coach does things in his or her own way. What your coach did last year might not be what your coach this year does.

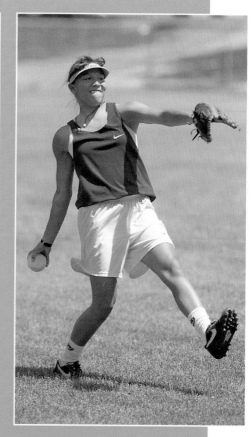

Doing the Crow Hop

For more power, some players take a little step with the ball-hand foot before doing a regular overhand throw.

Rachael is doing this move, called a crow hop, in the photos on this page. First, she fields the ball. She faces her target and takes a short step forward with her ball-hand leg. She hops on her ball-hand leg. She brings her throwing arm back. Her wrist is cocked. As her arm comes forward, Rachael shifts her weight to her glove-hand foot. She lets go of the ball in front of her body. Her throwing hand finishes just above her knee.

● *Sidearm*

Infielders use the sidearm throw when they need to make a quick throw. Molly is doing a sidearm throw in the photos on this page. Her forearm is parallel to the ground as she brings the ball back and then forward. She follows through across her body.

● *Snap throw*

A snap throw, below, is used when infielders have a runner trapped between the bases.

● *Underhand*

A player can quickly toss the ball from a crouch with an underhand throw. In the photos

on these two pages, Dupe is close to a teammate. Her teammate is standing on a

base. Dupe gently tosses the ball so her teammate can catch it. She doesn't flip the ball or let it spin off her fingers. If she did, the ball might sail over her teammate's head.

PITCHING

Good pitching is more than just tossing the ball underhand to the batter. A good pitcher must be able to throw the ball in the strike zone. But a pitcher also has to fool the batter.

A good pitcher knows that some batters will get hits. But the pitcher trusts the fielders to make the plays. Fielders can't help a pitcher who walks batter after batter. But a good pitcher also knows that everyone makes mistakes. If the pitcher walks a batter or allows a home run, the pitcher has to "shake it off." The pitcher also has to stay focused on pitching, even if a fielder makes a bad play.

In slow-pitch softball, the ball's arc must be at least 3 feet above the point of release. The ball can't go higher than 12 feet above the ground. An umpire will warn a pitcher if the pitches are too fast.

In fast-pitch, the softball can't have an arc of more than 3 feet. Fast-pitch pitchers are allowed to throw the ball as fast as they can. In fast-pitch, the faster, the better.

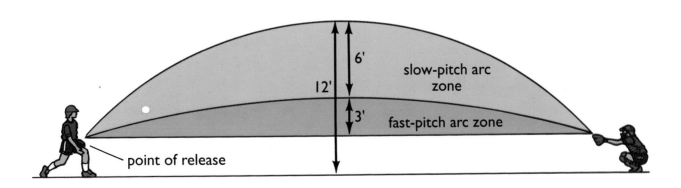

6'

12'

3'

slow-pitch arc zone

fast-pitch arc zone

point of release

Slow-Pitch Delivery

In the photos on this page and the next, Kathy shows how to pitch in slow-pitch softball. She starts with her ball-hand foot on the pitcher's rubber. Her other foot is behind the rubber. Her front foot can't leave the rubber until the ball is released.

Kathy grips the ball with her fingers. She holds the ball in front of her chest for at least two seconds. Then she swings her arm back.

Kathy steps forward as she swings her arm forward. She lets go of the ball just in front of her hip. Then she gets ready to field.

Pitching Warmup

Warming up your pitching arm is the first step in being a good pitcher. Start by running. On a cool day, wear a jacket. That keeps your body heat near your arm. Next, gently toss the ball underhand. Then, toss it overhand. This stretches muscles in your back, shoulder, and forearm.

Once you begin to practice pitching, make sure that you're the right distance from your catcher. Start pitching at half speed. Gradually speed up the pitches.

Fast-Pitch Delivery

There are two types of deliveries in fast-pitch: the slingshot and the windmill. The slingshot starts out like a slow-pitch delivery because the pitcher swings back the arm. But then, the pitcher whips the arm forward and releases the ball.

Most pitchers can throw the ball faster when they use the windmill. The windmill got its name from old-time pitchers, who would whirl their arms around and around to confuse the batter. Current rules allow only one circle.

● Slingshot

Rachael is demonstrating the slingshot in the photos on the next three pages. She begins with her ball-hand heel on top of the rubber. The toe of her other foot is against the back of the rubber. Rachael holds the ball with two or three fingers. Rachael holds both hands down and in front of her body for at least one second. Then

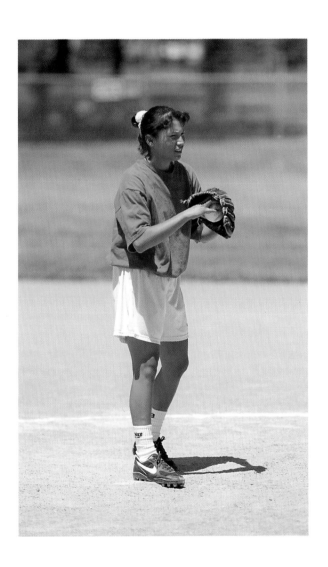 

Rachael brings the ball out of her glove. She swings her arm behind her so that the ball is above and behind her head. As she does that, she steps forward with her glove-hand foot.

This side view shows how high above her head Rachael brings the ball during the slingshot.

Rachael steps forward but keeps her weight on her back foot. Then, when she whips her arm forward, she shifts her weight forward. She plants her foot just before she lets go of

Rachael's arm goes up and across her body in the follow-through. She lands with her front foot pointing directly toward the batter. Then, since the ball could be hit right back at her, she quickly gets into fielding position.

the ball. As she lets go of the ball, she snaps her wrist. The wrist snap adds speed and spin to the ball. Because Rachael shifts her weight, her back foot comes off the mound.

● *Windmill*

The windmill is the most common delivery for fast-pitch pitchers. The illustration below

her glove. She does this the same way she would if she were doing the slingshot. She

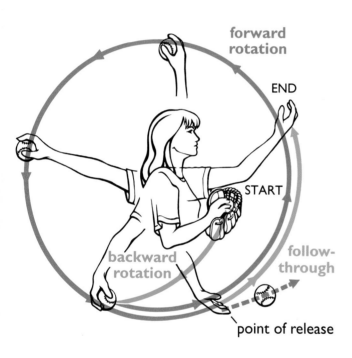

forward rotation

END

START

backward rotation

follow-through

point of release

The Windmill Delivery

shows the path of the ball during a windmill delivery. Notice that the ball goes in a complete circle. On this page and the next three pages, Leah shows how to do this move.

First, Leah starts by bringing the ball back and down out of

swings the ball down to her hip. Then Leah brings her arm forward. She shifts her weight to the ball-side foot. Leah swings the ball in front of her and above her head. At the same

time, she starts to step forward, keeping her weight back. When the ball is at its highest point, Leah's leg is fully extended. Leah swings the ball behind her and forward. Just after the ball passes her thigh, she releases it. She snaps her wrist forward as she lets go of the ball. Her front foot hits the ground as she shifts her weight completely to her front foot. After the release, her back foot leaves the pitcher's rubber. Her arm swings up smoothly in the follow-through. Then she quickly steps forward into fielding position.

This straight-ahead view shows Leah releasing the ball just as her hand passes her thigh.

The drop ball grip

The rise ball grip

The curveball grip

Stuff

By using different grips, a pitcher can make the ball spin in unusual ways. This is called putting stuff on the ball. Instead of going directly across the plate, balls with stuff move up, down, or sideways. The most common pitches are called the **rise ball, drop ball,** and **curveball.** A fourth pitch, called the **changeup,** is usually a slow drop or rise ball. The changeup fools batters who are expecting a fast pitch. The key to a good changeup is to make the delivery look like a fast pitch.

Several grips are shown at left. Each pitcher starts with these basic grips and then changes them to suit his or her style. Learning how to put stuff on the ball takes a lot of practice.

A drop ball spins toward the batter and then drops suddenly as it nears the plate. The faster the pitch, the more sharply the ball will drop.

A rise ball rolls off the pitcher's fingertips with back spin. A curveball curves away from a righthanded batter.

Hot Stuff

Lisa Fernandez was a star pitcher on the U.S. women's team that won a gold medal in the 1996 Olympics. Lisa wasn't such a star in her first game as a pitcher. She was eight years old and she walked 20 batters. Her team lost 28-0. Lisa could have given up on softball. Instead, she decided that she would do better next time. And she did.

Lisa kept playing softball. She played all through high school and college. She kept getting better. She went to the University of California at Los Angeles. In her four years there, she struck out 709 batters. Lisa led UCLA to four Women's College World Series. She and her teammates won NCAA championships twice. They were runners-up the other two years. After she graduated, Lisa played for one of the top fast-pitch teams in the country.

Chapter 5

HITTING AND RUNNING

What's the most fun part of softball? Well, many players think there's nothing like hitting! Everyone likes to smack the ball as hard as possible and watch it fly. Racing around the bases is exciting. And, everyone loves to score runs. Master these skills and you'll be scoring runs!

Hitting

● Grip

Just like throwing and pitching, hitting begins with the right grip. In the photos at right, Leah is gripping the bat. The hand knuckles of her top hand line up with the finger knuckles of her bottom hand.

On the left, Leah shows the regular way to grip a bat. On the right, she shows how to choke up on the bat. Players choke up when a pitcher is throwing very fast, the bat they're using is too heavy, or they want to have an exceptionally quick swing.

53

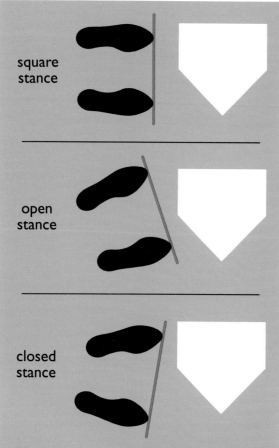

square
stance

open
stance

closed
stance

High-Powered Footwork

Most players learn to hit with their feet in the parallel, or square, stance. Both toes point directly at the plate. As they become better hitters, some players use the open stance. In this stance, the batter moves the front foot away from the plate. Players use this stance when they want to hit the ball to the same side of the field that they are standing on. (That's leftfield for a righthanded batter.) When a batter wants to hit the ball to the other side of the field, he or she might use a closed stance. (That's leftfield for a lefthanded batter.) In a closed stance, the batter moves the front foot closer to the plate.

● *Stance*

Leah shows how to swing the bat in the photos on this page and the next two pages. Leah stands with her feet about shoulder width apart. She bends her knees a little bit. She holds the bat off her shoulder and behind her ear.

Leah holds her arms out from her body. She keeps her shoulders level.

● *Swing*

As the pitcher releases the ball, Leah shifts her weight to her back foot. Her shoulders turn back slightly, as if she were coiling her body like a spring. Leah steps toward the pitcher with her front foot. Leah's hips turn slightly as she swings the bat but her back foot stays put.

Curing Pop Ups

Pop ups are high fly balls that are easy to catch. If you hit pop ups, ask your coach or a friend to watch your stride. Your stride is the step you take toward the pitcher while swinging the bat. If you take a stride that's too long, you might hit a pop up. Try taking a smaller step. End with your front leg straight.

Practice Drills for Hitting

Major league baseball players hit off tees to practice their swings. Colleen is working on her swing in the photo above.

The soft toss drill that Colleen and Dupe are doing below is another sure winner. Stand close to a fence, as Dupe is. Have someone toss the ball just a little in front of you. Swing hard and smash it into the fence.

As the bat hits the ball, Leah snaps her wrists. Her front leg is straight and her back leg is bent. Leah rolls her wrists over as she swings the bat. She keeps swinging the bat until her hands are near her front shoulder.

To use all her power, Leah hits the ball before it crosses home plate. That way she can stretch out her arms fully. If she waited for the ball to cross the plate, she wouldn't have time to extend her arms. She wants to hit the ball when it is two or three feet in front of the plate.

● Bunting

The ball bounces off the bat. It rolls a few feet from home plate and stops. Two or three fielders rush to the ball. Who's going to throw it? Batters who know how to **bunt** can cause this confusion.

Batters aren't allowed to bunt in slow-pitch. In fast-pitch, though, bunting is a big part of the game. Most batters don't bunt if they have two strikes. With two strikes, a foul bunt will count as the third strike.

There are two kinds of bunts. A player would hit a **sacrifice bunt** to move a runner to the next base. It's called a sacrifice because the batter often will be thrown out at first base.

In the photos at right, Tripper demonstrates a sacrifice bunt. When the pitcher begins her pitch, Tripper turns to face her.

Tripper slides his top hand along the bat. His thumb is on the bottom and his fingers are curled on the top. Instead of swinging, Tripper taps the ball with the bat. He pushes the ball into the dirt.

A player would use a **drag bunt** to reach first base safely. The basic movement for the drag bunt is like that for the sacrifice bunt. The big difference is in the timing. Molly is doing a drag bunt in the photos above. She stands in the batter's box as though she will swing. Once the pitch is in the air, she quickly shifts into the bunting stance. She grips the bat the same way Tripper did for the sacrifice bunt. As Molly taps the ball into the dirt, she starts running to first base. That head start gives Molly a chance to get on base.

Running the Bases

Every team needs smart baserunners. Every player on base should know the count, the number of outs, and the score. Knowing these things will help the baserunner decide what to do when the ball is hit. The baserunner will also get help from the coaches standing near first and third bases. These base coaches will watch the ball. The base coaches will tell the baserunner whether to slide, come in standing up, or try for another base.

● Getting to First

After she hits the ball, Dupe, at right, steps toward first base with her back foot. She does that because she shifted her weight to her front foot during the swing.

Dupe doesn't stop to watch the ball. She runs as fast as she can. She doesn't slow down once she gets to the base because runners are allowed to run past first base. Dupe runs straight across the bag.

Dropped Third Strike Rule

Three strikes and you're out, right? Not always in fast-pitch softball. If the catcher drops the third strike, the batter can try to beat the throw to first base. The batter can run if first base is empty. Or, the batter can run if there are already two outs, even if there's a baserunner on first base.

If Dupe thinks she has hit an **extra-base hit,** she veers out on the way to first base. She touches the inside of the base with her foot as she turns toward second.

● *Stealing*

Just as there is no bunting in slow-pitch, there's no stealing either. A baserunner could get too much of a head start while the slow pitch was on its way to the plate. In fast-pitch, a base-runner can try to steal a base

as soon as the ball leaves the pitcher's hand.

A baserunner can't leave the base before the ball leaves the pitcher's hand. But a baserunner can start with one foot behind the base, as Colleen is doing in the photos above. As the pitcher reaches the highest point of the delivery, Colleen strides forward with her back leg. Colleen's other foot stays on the bag until the ball leaves the pitcher's hand.

● *The Slide*

The fielder is going to try to tag the baserunner. How does the baserunner avoid making an out? By sliding under or around the tag. A baserunner might also slide to avoid overrunning second or third base. Instead of slowing down, the baserunner slides to a stop.

A baserunner needs to decide early to slide, and then he or she must slide. Beginning a slide late or changing your mind once you've started to slide can cause an injury.

Most baserunners use the straight-in, or bent-leg, slide that Colleen is doing on the photos on this page and the next page. Colleen begins her slide when she is 10 to 12 feet from the base. She bends her knees, which drops her hips. Then Colleen puts one leg toward the bag. She tucks the other leg under the opposite knee. She slides on her hip and the upper part of her thigh. She keeps her arms up to avoid hurting them.

Chapter 6

TAKING THE FIELD

After all the conditioning and practice, it's time to play against another team. That's when the fun really begins!

Here's a tip for when you're out on the field. Take a deep breath. Then think about softball's two unwritten rules: Do your best and have fun!

Positions

Nine people take the field in softball. Six positions are in the infield. These are: pitcher, catcher, shortstop, first, second, and third base. The other three positions are in the outfield: rightfield, leftfield, and centerfield. Some slow-pitch softball leagues allow a 10th fielder. This fielder plays in the outfield.

Conduct on the Field

Being a good sport is as important as being a good hitter or fielder. How can you show your sportsmanship?

Don't kick dirt or throw your glove, hat, or bat. Don't say mean things to your teammates or opponents. Don't argue with the umpire. You won't agree with every call—no player ever does—but making the calls is the umpire's job and making the plays is yours.

Do cheer for your teammates by saying things like "Nice pitch." You can tease your opponents by yelling "Easy out." Just be prepared. Some players will respond by hitting the ball over the fence. After all, that's what you'll do, right?

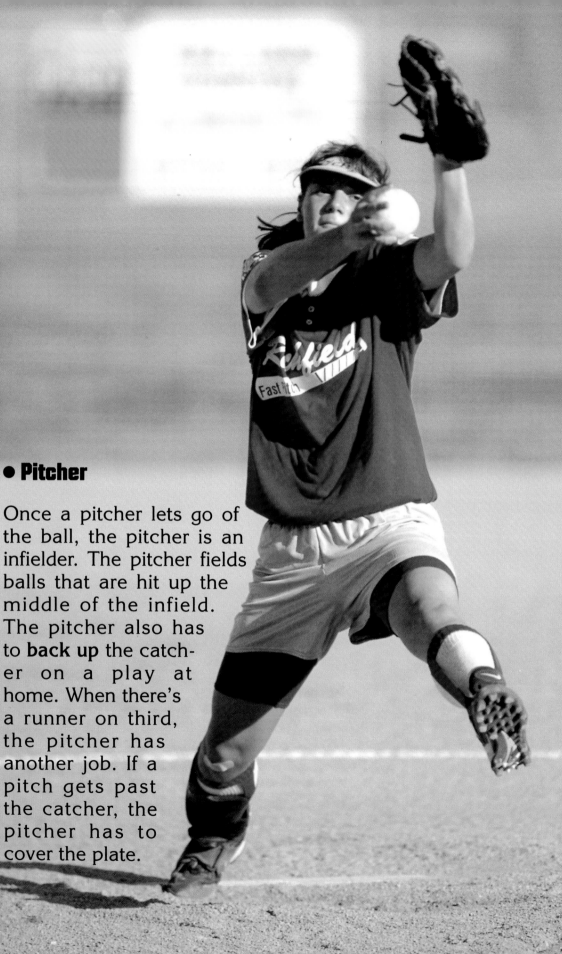

● Pitcher

Once a pitcher lets go of the ball, the pitcher is an infielder. The pitcher fields balls that are hit up the middle of the infield. The pitcher also has to **back up** the catcher on a play at home. When there's a runner on third, the pitcher has another job. If a pitch gets past the catcher, the pitcher has to cover the plate.

● *Catcher*

Catchers need to be quick, tough, and flexible. They lead the defense. Catchers study the other team's batters for strengths and weaknesses. Catchers make sure everyone on their team knows the count and number of outs. Catchers also know when and how to cheer up their pitcher.

In fast-pitch softball, catchers have more jobs. The catcher decides what kind of pitch the pitcher should throw. Katie, in

the bottom photo at left, shows how she signals this to her pitcher. To give the sign, Katie squats. She uses her fingers to send a series of signals. Her hand is between her legs so that the other team's players can't tell what pitch will be thrown. Then Katie holds up her mitt to give the pitcher a target. Katie puts her bare hand behind her back to protect it.

Once a batter makes it onto the base paths, the catcher watches for the steal. After she signals the pitcher, the catcher moves into position. Her legs are bent at the knee almost as though she's sitting in a chair. She bends forward and extends her mitt. If she thinks she can throw the ball to second base before the baserunner can get there, she throws it.

When a runner is on base, Katie's most important job is to make sure the ball doesn't get past her. If the pitcher throws the ball in the dirt, Katie blocks the ball. She falls to her knees and puts the tip of her glove in the dirt. She leans forward so the ball won't bounce over her shoulder.

● *First Base*

Like Tamara in the photos on this page, the person playing first is often tall. Those added inches can help when catching a high throw.

When a teammate is throwing the ball to her, Tamara puts her bare-hand foot on the corner of the bag. She stretches toward the teammate throwing the ball. Tamara's most important job is to catch the ball so it doesn't get past her. Tamara moves off the base if she has to in order to catch the ball.

In the photos on this page, Molly is the shortstop. When the batter hits a pop fly in Molly's direction, she calls out that she'll catch it. Then, she runs to get underneath the ball while the leftfielder backs up the play.

● *Second Base and Shortstop*

Both infielders at second base and shortstop need to be good fielders. Many balls are hit up the middle of the infield.

When a runner reaches second base, that runner is in **scoring position.** The fielders on either side of second have to know who is going to cover the base on every play.

In general, when the ball is hit to the rightfield side of second, the fielder at second fields the ball. The shortstop covers the base. If the ball is hit to the left-field side of second, the fielder at second goes to the base. The shortstop fields the ball.

● *Third Base*

The fielder at third base has to be able to field bunts. This fielder also has to be able to catch line drives, like the fielder is in the photo at right.

In the photos below, Kathy shows how to tag out a base-runner. She straddles the base. She holds the ball with her bare hand inside the pocket of her glove. She puts her glove on the ground in front of the base. She lets the runner slide into it.

Hitting the Cutoff

When the ball is hit deep into the out-field, fielders use the cutoff play. A ball can be returned to the infield more rapidly by two short throws than by one long throw.

In the example in the photos above, a ball is hit to Colleen in centerfield. The shortstop, Molly, races to a spot in a straight line between centerfield and home plate. Colleen throws the ball to Molly. Molly catches the ball. She turns and quickly throws the ball to Tripper at home plate.

● *Outfield*

Outfielders need speed, fielding ability, and strong arms. The centerfielder needs the most speed. Centerfield is the largest area to cover. The leftfielder needs to be ready for hits down the third base line. The right-fielder must have a strong arm to throw the ball to third base.

Outfielders also have to back up their teammates in case the ball gets past the first fielder. When the ball is hit toward the leftfielder or rightfielder, the centerfielder backs up that player. When the ball is hit to the centerfielder, the outfielder closest to the play backs up the centerfielder.

Even when the ball doesn't make it into the outfield, the outfielders must back up each play in case of a bad throw. For example, the centerfielder backs up the fielder at second on a throw from the catcher.

Outfielders decide where to stand by thinking of several factors. Some of these factors are whether the batter is right- or lefthanded and the batter's size.

The Game

Let's get an idea of how the skills and moves presented in this book are used in a game. We'll follow the Maroons and the Golds in the seventh inning of their game. The Maroons have six runs. The Golds have five.

Before the seventh inning starts, Katie catches Leah's final practice pitch. Katie throws the ball to Allison at second base. Then she yells "Let's go Maroon! Three up. Three down."

The first batter for the Golds steps into the batter's box. Katie signals Leah to throw a drop ball. Leah's arm rotates up and back in the windmill. She releases the ball. The Golds batter swings. The ball spins high into the air.

Katie rips the mask off her face. She looks up to see the ball. It's coming down to her right. Katie tosses her mask to her left so she won't trip over it. Her bare hand follows the ball into her mitt. One out.

Dorothy is the Golds next batter. Katie signals a rise ball.

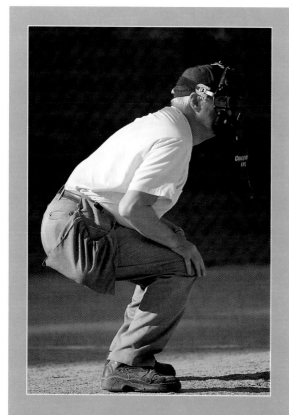

Behind the Plate

Umpires enforce the rules of the game. The home plate umpire stands behind the catcher and wears a face mask and chest protector. The home plate umpire calls balls and strikes. This umpire also decides if a hit is fair or foul. The base umpires decide if a batter is safe or out.

Leah throws one. Dorothy swings. "Strike one!" the umpire shouts.

On the next pitch, Dorothy hits the ball up the middle of the infield. Dorothy is safe at first base.

As Anne leaves the **on-deck circle**, the Maroons covering first and third move closer to home plate. With Dorothy on first, the Maroons think Anne might try to hit a sacrifice bunt. Sure enough, Anne shifts into the bunting stance.

Anne taps the ball into the dirt toward third base. It dribbles over the white chalk line. "Foul ball!" the umpire roars.

Anne walks back to the plate. She picks up her bat. Leah throws another fast pitch. But instead of bunting, Anne smacks a line drive past third base. The leftfielder runs to reach the ball. Meanwhile, Dorothy scores. The third base coach motions Anne to run home. Anne starts to slide when she is several strides from home. Her feet slide under Katie's mitt. The umpire signals that she is safe.

Katie hands the ball to Leah, who had backed up the play. "Shake it off," Katie tells Leah. "Let's get the next two batters."

Leah takes a deep breath as she walks out to the rubber. The next two Golds batters hit the ball, but the Maroon fielders make the outs. After the third out, Katie dashes to the dugout. She quickly takes off her chest protector and shin guards. She's at the top of the **batting order.**

Katie steps into the batter's box. She watches the ball. She sees it hit her bat. The ball flies over the backstop.

The second pitch looks high and outside to Katie so she doesn't swing. The umpire calls it a strike. Two strikes on Katie. The Maroon fans groan. Katie steps out of the box. She takes a practice swing.

On the next pitch, Katie swings and taps a blooper over the shortstop's head. The ball drops between the infield and outfield for a single.

Next, Mary hits the ball up the middle. The third base coach holds up Katie at third. Mary has a stand-up double.

The Golds pitcher walks the next batter. The bases are

loaded. Then Leah steps up to the plate. She hits a hard fly ball between the rightfielder and the centerfielder. The runner on first doesn't think that the ball will be caught. She doesn't **tag up.** She starts running to second base.

Dorothy dives and catches the ball. She rolls to her feet and throws to first base. The ball beats the runner back to first. Two outs! But Katie had tagged up at third on the fly ball. She runs home to score. The game is tied.

Leah and Katie cheer as Mary goes to third on a **wild pitch.** The Golds pitcher throws two strikes to Diane.

Then Diane drives the next pitch between second and third. The fielder at third leaps to catch the ball. But the ball bounces off the top of her glove. The leftfielder picks up the ball and fires it to first. Thud. Slap. Diane beats the throw by a split second. Mary scores. The Maroons win! The two teams walk to the center of the field to shake hands.

Softball Talk

arc: The vertically curved path of a pitch to the plate.

back up: To get behind the fielder who is going to make the catch, in case the ball gets past him or her.

ball: A pitch that doesn't pass through the strike zone and at which the batter doesn't swing.

batting order: The set order in which the team bats. Players may not bat out of order, but substitutions are allowed.

bunt: A softly hit ball.

changeup: An intentionally slow pitch that is thrown with the same motion as a fast pitch to fool the batter.

count: The number of balls and strikes against a batter. The number of balls is always given first. So if the umpire has called two strikes and the pitcher has also thrown three balls, the count is 3-and-2—three balls and two strikes.

curveball: A pitch that curves toward or away from a batter.

drag bunt: A bunt that a batter disguises until the last possible moment. A drag bunt is used when the batter is trying to reach base safely.

drop ball: A ball that moves sharply down as it approaches the plate.

extra-base hit: A hit that allows the batter to advance past first base.

A *double* gets the batter to second base, a *triple* to third, and a *home run* to home plate.

fly ball: A ball that is hit high into the air in fair territory.

force-out: A situation in which a baserunner must go to the next base, but the fielder holding the ball touches the base before the runner. A force-out, also called a force play, can only happen at first base or when all the bases behind the runner are occupied.

foul ball: A batted ball that lands outside the foul lines.

ground ball: A batted ball that rolls on the ground. Also called a grounder.

infield: The area between the bases, usually dirt or sand.

line drive: A hard-hit ball that travels on a straight, relatively low path.

on-deck circle: The area, often outlined with chalk, where the next batter in the order waits.

out: The failure of a batter or runner to reach a base safely. A team is allowed three outs in an inning.

outfield: The grassy area between the bases and the fence.

pitcher's rubber: The rectangle set in the middle of the infield where the pitcher must stand when delivering the ball.

pocket: The webbing of a glove between the thumb and forefinger.

rise ball: A pitch that moves upward sharply as it approaches the plate.

sacrifice bunt: A play in which the batter bunts and is put out but succeeds in moving a teammate at least one base. The batter's team must have fewer than two outs.

scoring position: A baserunner on second or third base is in scoring position.

strike: A pitch that passes through the strike zone without being hit. Also, a pitch that is hit foul when the batter has fewer than two strikes.

strikeout: An out that results from the batter being charged with three strikes.

strike zone: The invisible area over home plate through which the pitch must pass to be called a strike.

stuff: The adjusting of a pitch so that it drops, rises, or curves.

tag: An out a fielder makes by touching a runner with the ball.

tag up: The act of touching one's original base, after a fielder catches a fly ball, in order to be able to go to the next base.

walk: A free pass to first base, awarded to a batter who takes four balls without being put out by a strikeout or a fielder. Also called a base on balls.

wild pitch: A pitch well outside the strike zone that is difficult for the catcher to block or catch.

FURTHER READING

Dickson, Paul. *The Worth Book of Softball: A Celebration of America's True National Pastime.* New York: Facts on File, 1994.

Gutman, Bill. *Softball for Boys and Girls: Start Right and Play Well.* New York: Marshall Cavendish, 1990.

Kneer, Marian E. and Charles L. McCord. *Softball: Slow and Fast Pitch.* Dubuque, Iowa: Brown & Benchmark, 1995.

Potter, Diane L. *Softball: Steps to Success.* Champaign, Ill.: Human Kinetics Publishers, Inc., 1989.

Walker, Dick. *Softball: A Step-By-Step Guide.* Mahwah, N.J.: Troll Associates, 1990.

FOR MORE INFORMATION

Amateur Softball Association
2801 N.E. 50th Street
Oklahoma City, OK 73111

Cinderella Softball Leagues
P. O. Box 1411
Corning, NY 14830

INDEX

Amateur Softball Association (ASA), 10, 11, 13

ball, 20
baserunning, 59; getting to first, 59–60; sliding, 62–63; stealing, 60-61
bases, 14, 20–21
batter's box, 14, 20
batting: bunt, 57–58; grip, 53; practice, 56; stance, 54; swing, 55–56
batting order, 75
beep baseball, 11
bunt: drag, 58; sacrifice, 57

catcher, 67–68; blocking balls, 68; equipment, 17, 19; signals, 68
catcher's mitt, 17
centerfielder, 72
changeup, 50
Chicago World's Fair, 10
choke up, 53
coaches, 33, 59, 74
conduct on the field, 65
count, 20
crow hop, 34
curveball, 50
cutoff, 72

diamond. *See* field
diamond drill, 24
drop ball, 50

equipment, 10, 19; ball, 9, 16–17; bat, 18; batting helmet, 18, 19; cleats, 19; glove, 17
extra-base hit, 60

fair ball, 14

fair territory, 20
fast-pitch softball, 11, 39, 57, 66, 68, 69, 70; pitching, 42–49
Fernandez, Lisa, 51
field, 14, 15
fielder's glove, 17
fielding: fly balls, 23-25; ground balls, 25, 26; line drives, 28; practice, 23, 24, 27, 29
first base, 14, 20, 21
first base position, 69
Fischer, Leo, 10
fly ball, 21, 23–25
force-out, 21
foul ball, 14
foul lines, 14
foul territory, 20

game, 73–76

Hancock, George, 8–9
hitting. *See* batting
home plate, 14

Indoor Base Ball, 9
infield, 14
infielders, 69–71
innings, 21

leftfielder, 72

mush ball, 9

Olympic Games, 9, 51
on-deck circle, 74
out, 20, 21
outfield, 14, 72
outfielder, 72

pitcher, 39, 66

pitching, 39, 66; fast-pitch, 42–49; slingshot, 42–45; slow-pitch, 40–41; stuff, 11, 50; warmup, 41; windmill, 42, 46–49
pop up, 55
positions, 65
pumpkin ball, 9

Richardson, Dot, 9
rightfielder, 72
rise ball, 50
Rober, Lewis, 8, 9
rubber, 14, 40, 42, 48
rules, 9, 10, 20–21
run, 21

scoring position, 70
second base, 14, 21
second base position, 70
shortstop, 9, 70
slingshot, 42–45

slow-pitch softball, 11, 39, 57; pitching, 40–41
softball, history of, 7–10
strike, 20, 59
strike zone, 20

tag, 21, 62, 71
tag up, 76
third base, 14, 21
third base position, 71
throwing, 30; overhand, 30–33; practice, 33; sidearm, 35; snap throw, 36; underhand, 36–37

umpire, 14, 20, 65, 74

walk, 20
warmup, 29, 41
wild pitch, 76
windmill, 42, 46–49